I0438005

Ol' Forked Horn

C. R. Autrey

iUniverse, Inc.
New York   Bloomington

Ol' Forked Horn

iUniverse books may be ordered through booksellers or by contacting:

iUniverse
1663 Liberty Drive
Bloomington, IN 47403
www.iuniverse.com
1-800-Authors (1-800-288-4677)

ISBN: 978-1-4401-2048-0 (pbk)
ISBN: 978-1-4401-2049-7 (ebk)

Printed in the United States of America

iUniverse rev. date: 02/24/2009

Acknowledgments

I am thankful to my daddy for taking the time to teach me the skills of squirrel hunting, and to Earl Sims who taught me the art of deer hunting, and to my mother for cooking almost anything that I killed. To my family and friends for encouraging and supporting me in my endeavor to write this book. To my many deer hunting buddies. To my son, Scott Autrey, for the cover illustrations. To my wife for reading and editing this manuscript. I am thankful to God for allowing me to grow up during a time when the art of deer hunting with dogs was an enjoyed sport—and for giving me the grace to be able to write about it.

Dedication

To all of you who had dogs that you fed and took care of for twelve months; although you only got to hunt with them for six weeks out of the year, and you spent a lot of looking for them and hoping they had not gotten shot, lost, or stolen. It was a joyful time when you went back to the place where you had turned your hounds loose, and as you began calling for them, Ol' Sally, Tom, or Joe would come out from the bushes, wagging his or her tail. Then you would take your dogs home and feed them and yourself, knowing that you had already missed the ballgame. But I would take deer hunting with dogs over any ballgame. It was all worth it when you turned the dogs loose the next morning and they jumped a deer. When the deer headed to the stander, the stander would strain his ear so hard that he could hear a red bug sliding down a blade of grass. Your heart would be pounding and your mouth would be getting dryer by the minute. A breaking stick or a shaking bush and the deer would be in shooting range. In that split second, you had to be sure it was a legal deer and shoot, or it would be gone. Shooting from a tree stand can't compare. This is what I call deer hunting, and I will be ready again tomorrow, will you?

Prologue

I was born in the late thirties, a time when hunting was just a way of life and I grew up hunting game to put food on the table.

As the game laws changed, hunting for me became less of a fun sport. The new laws only allowed you to take buckshot on a hunt. You could not have buckshot and small shot at the same time. The old laws said you could not sit or stand on tree limbs or planks that were off the ground, but the new law allowed tree stands.

I thought that I could outsmart any critter that walked, but Ol' Forked Horn was the greatest challenge I ever faced.

Contents

The Fool-proof Plan

It all happened with one phone call from John. The Champions were having a deer drive, and they wanted me to go. Nowadays, deer hunting with dogs is a thing of the past, but that was how it was done back then in this part of Southern Alabama.

They planned the hunt for next Saturday, which was the last day of deer season. John said that the Smiths, who lived across Black Creek from Campbell Town, were having trouble with deer eating the peas and turnips that they had planted. They said the deer were even trying to dig up the sweet potatoes.

The Smith brothers farmed and did odd jobs for a living. They probably made a little moonshine, too. They lived in the old Stave Mill houses long after the Stave Mill was gone. These houses were built from scrap lumber, and the wooden windows opened and shut like real doors. You opened them to let the sunlight in and closed them at night to keep out bugs and cold winds. The yards were bare of grass and were well kept. The women would go out into the woods and cut dogwood sprouts, which they would tie together to make yard brooms. They would use these brooms to keep the yard swept neat. These were hard-working people, and for the most part, they were happy—but they were also suspicious.

I promised John that I would make an effort to scout the area where we wanted to hunt and I would see him Saturday. I never like to hunt an area without scouting it out first. I am pushing my seventieth birthday now. Sometimes, when I stop to think, I forget to start again; but back then, I could remember almost everything that went on in an area when I scouted it. I started thinking about the dogs and the best way to stop them if they got away from the hunters.

I got up early in the morning to head for the Smith's farm and get started scouting the hunting area. I reached for and got the lightest shotgun that I had, an old 16 ga single barrel that had belonged to my granddaddy. I filled my hunting coat pockets with 16 ga shells, jumped into my old Chevrolet pickup truck, and headed out. It was about ten miles, more or less, down a farm-to-market blacktop road that farmers used to market their goods. My old truck was a dry-weather truck. It would go almost anywhere in dry weather but often got stuck during the wet season.

This time of year, most of the leaves had fallen from the trees. However, less than a month ago, they had outdone themselves with colors that only God could have painted.

As I traveled down the road, I started to think of the past and a creek where I had once caught a rabbit. I remembered that it had rained for over a week and water was all over the place. Although the rain had stopped, it was turning colder by the hour. This was a good time to coon hunt. Two other coon hunters and I had headed down the creek when the hounds struck a fresh coon trail. With so much water, it was hard for the dogs to track a coon, but we followed them as they made a wide circle. We stopped for a moment to listen to hear which way the hounds would go, and then we realized they were heading toward us. This upset a rabbit, and he ran straight toward us. The only way he had to go was in the puddle of water, which looked to be only two or three inches deep. As the rabbit started to swim, for some strange reason, I stepped into the puddle to catch the rabbit. This was definitely not a wise choice. The puddle was three-feet deep, and one of my pant legs got wet and my boot was filled with water. By the time we got back to the truck, my pant leg was frozen solid, and my feet were cold. Needless to say, we called in the dogs and let Mr. Ringtail have the water holes.

Driving on, I could see birds trying to find their dinner and a chipmunk running across the road with its mouth filled with acorns. When I got to the turnoff road, it was dusty and rough.

I forded a small stream. This stream started from a spring that flowed year round with the coldest water you have ever tasted. Years ago, the Stave Mill women would take their clothes to this same stream and wash them. There were still signs of ashes where they had built fires under the wash pots.

I stopped to get a drink of water and maybe wash the dust out of my mouth. As I was thinking back on all the history of this place, I found a token by the ashes. In times past, tokens were used to pay the people who worked at the Stave Mill. These Tokens could only be redeemed at the Stave Mill Commissary Store.

As I drove on, there were the small fields and the old houses. John Henry and his brother were digging sweet taters. I stopped to talk with John Henry and told him about our plans to rid them of their pests. He was excited about it as he called over his brother Jim to tell him about our plan. Jim said he would shake my hand, but that he had so much tater sap on his hands, we might stick together. I asked Jim if it hurt his back to pick those taters, but he said, "You see how short I am, I'm closer to 'em than you are. It don't bother me much." John Henry—who was always suspicious—said that we might kill one or two deer but that one called Ol' Forked Horn had outsmarted everyone who had hunted him. He said, "Ol' Forked Horn has fire in his eyes and blows smoke out of his nose. He can outthink any man."

I got his permission to hunt the land and to look for deer signs. The Smiths had to dig sweet taters and could not go with me. Jim told me to drive around the field to the old, log road. He said that would lead to the place where the hunt was to take place.

As I started walking back to my pickup, I heard Jim holler, "Stop before you get to the junkyard pool." I said, "OK," and drove off. I had driven about half a mile when, *there it was*, a big mud hole in the middle of the road.

Now, I knew why they called it the junkyard pool. You could see where trucks and jeeps had gotten stuck and how being pulled or winched out had taken a toll on the vehicles. There were bumpers, finders, headlights, and one tire lying about. The old pool had enough water to raise tons of mosquitoes.

After parking at the pool, I took my old 16 ga shotgun and started out on foot. Passing the mud hole, I walked up the hill to what at one time had been an old house place. There was a great, big, oak tree, loaded with acorns. Where there are acorns, there are squirrels. The leaf covered ground, made it hard to slip quietly up to the tree. I had spooked some squirrels, and they ran into a hollow tree.

I knew that to kill a squirrel, I would need to sit very still, and so I did. The squirrels started eating acorns again. I shot and killed three young ones and put them into my hunting coat. I could almost taste squirrel gravy.

I'm gonna tell you the best thing to do with a squirrel. First, you bend its tail over its back at the base of the tail and cut across the tail through the bone, leaving the top skin on. Step on the tail with your foot and pull upward with the back legs. The skin will slip off, down to the front feet and head. Cut off the feet and head. Draw out the innards. With that done, wash and cut the squirrel into pieces. Then, put enough oil in a pan to cover the bottom. Take your cut pieces and dredge them in flour. Add salt and black pepper. Brown the meat and add enough water to make gravy. While your squirrel is cooking, you need to bake some biscuits.

Here is a good receipt for making biscuits: Take thirteen tablespoons self-rising flour and add two tablespoons of Crisco. Mix and then add enough buttermilk to mix into dough that you separate and roll into round biscuits. Bake these at five hundred degrees for twelve minutes.

As I sat down by the old oak tree, I could see across a clear-cut that covered a wide area near a small stream. The bottomland had been farmed years ago. (A clear-cut is where the loggers cut everything, big and small.) They had left only the trees along the creek bank, which was strewn with many limbs and treetops. This was good cover for the deer to hide or bend down. On the other side of the clear-cut was a log road. That is where the hunters were to stand and wait for the deer to run past. These types of hunters are called standers. I decided to stand by the big oak.

At this point, the area had been scouted, and the plan was made for the big hunt. On my way home and as I neared the end of the dirt road, I remembered a little country store with a gristmill. The gristmill is where, every other Saturday, they ground meal from the corn that the farmers bring in. A black man called Big Sam and his wife owned the store. I stopped by to get a coke and candy bar. In these parts of the south, we always stop for a coke, which most of the time meant an orange soda or Mountain Dew. I told Big Sam about our hunting plans for Saturday so that he could stock up on nick-knacks for the hunters. Big Sam said that was all the hunters would eat if they thought they could kill Ol' Forked Horn.

As tales of the big, blue buck started to grow, one man said, "He is as big as a mule. He whipped a pack of dogs. He got fire in his head and has been seen blowing smoke from his nose."

Another person said, "He done eat the Smith brothers out of their house and home. They never got a shot at him. He's like a goblin. People round here is afraid of him. Best leave that one be."

I bragged that we would be eating Mr. Forked Horn Saturday night—Big Sam's eyes rolled back in his head, and he had a good laugh at me.

He was still laughing when he asked if I wanted any fresh-ground cornmeal. He said he would be grinding this Saturday and would have some for sale. I sure did want some. It would make good dressing for New Year's dinner. Dressing and deer roast sounded tasty.

As I started for home, I could not help but think of all the good times we had had while hunting. We had coon dogs for hunting coon. If a coon ran up a tree, we would not shoot it in the tree. Someone would climb the tree and shake the coon out. Then the dogs would kill the coon. This saved money on shotgun shells. Back then, it was against the law to shoot a coon at night with a 22 ga rifle, anyway.

We had squirrel dogs, fox dogs, bird dogs, and yard dogs. We used dogs for everything. During hunting season, we hunted from river to river with our dogs, and no one cared.

Then came the *city hunters* with their money, and they bought all the good hunting land. They put up tree stands, planted green patches, or put out shelled corn. They started shooting our dogs if they crossed their hunting clubs. Ninety percent of the deer that they shot was after sundown. This was against the law, but money talks. Dog hunting took a backseat to tree standing. Today there are only a few days a year that you can hunt with dogs. While we hunted for the meat, it seemed that they didn't. It hurt us to see where they had left whole deer laying in the woods or where they had cut off the back legs and left the rest. Well, I have said enough about that.

Friday night, having a plan worked out in my head, I called John to share my idea with him. I would go to the big oak, and they could put the standers on the old-log road. Little John would turn their walker dogs loose on the north end of the clear-cut and Terry could turn his cur dogs loose on the south end of the clear-cut bottom. There would be dogs on both ends of the clear-cut and standers on the log road. I would be backing them up on the west side. No deer would want to face the farmer's yard dogs in the daylight anyway. It was a fool-proof plan, I thought. John liked the plan, and the hunt was on for the next day at seven AM.

The Hunt

I got up early on Saturday morning and thought to myself, *Show time, Mr. Forked Horn.* After feasting on a breakfast of squirrel gravy and biscuits, I grabbed my double-barrel 12 ga shotgun. My hunting coat was still in the pickup. My heart was pounding as I finally headed out to hunt Ol' Forked Horn. I checked my watch at least half-a-dozen times. I had plenty of time to get to the scrap iron pool and walk to the big oak.

As I turned onto the farm-to-market road, I was thinking of a turkey hunt several years ago. It really is as much fun getting ready to hunt as it is hunting. I had parked in the back of an old church where there was a cemetery. Sitting in my truck that morning, looking across the grave yard, at the grave markers, they seemed to move. As the dew on the church started to drip off the roof, it hit an old, five-gallon bucket with a thumping sound. This made the hair stand up on the back of my neck and almost ended the hunt before it started.

It started breaking daylight .I could see what was happening s I forced myself out of the truck and started walking to my lookout point. The trees were turning from what looked like black to green. You know it is day when the trees look green. Two owls were having a hooting contest. That was good because sometimes an owl hooting will make a turkey gobble.

I stopped under a tree where a turkey hen was roosting. The hen woke up putting and yelping. Old Tom gobbled back to the hen from more than two football fields away. Here came the turkey in full strut, gobbling. The hen flew down, and I had gotten ready to shoot when both turkeys flew away. They had not seen me. Puzzled, I sat still. Finally, I saw what had spooked my turkeys.

An old, faded-out-looking, red fox stood there looking disappointed. I could see by the color markings that the fox was a female. This one had a black tip on its tail. The male always has a white-tipped tail. As the fox started along, a rabbit jumped into the road. The race was on. I had never seen so much jumping and running. The fox won. With the rabbit in her mouth, she started back the way from which she had come. Moving along at a slow pace, I was trying to follow her so that she would not see me.

Red foxes rear their young starting in late January. By now, the puppies would still be eating meat caught by their mother. I lost sight of her and walked on until I spotted some mounds of sand where something had dug holes. I walked toward the biggest hole. There were bird feathers, rabbit hair, and numerous fox tracks, big and small. The mother fox darted out of the den. She was running away when another hunter—that I had not seen—shot and killed her. He thought the fox had gone mad and was trying to bite him. I hollered so that he wouldn't shoot me, too. We talked about what would happen to the little puppies. There was only one pup, and after we dug it out of the hole, I took him home with me.

I fed the fox puppy like he was a puppy dog. As he grew, he would play with me. We played hide-and-seek. I would hide, and he would track me down. I would climb a tree, and he would climb the tree after me. (Red fox can climb like cats, and unlike gray fox, they have hair under their feet.) I named the little fox Charlie, and although we had great fun together, I could not get the wild out of him. One day, my dad had Charlie on a leash. They were walking past the chicken pen, and this scared the little chicks. One flew past Charlie, and Charlie caught the little chick in midair. After that, my mother made me keep Charlie penned up. One day, Charlie broke out of the cage. Seeing his chance for freedom, he ran into the woods. I thought Charlie was gone for good. One morning, about three weeks later, I heard my mother yelling. I thought she had seen a snake, and I ran to her. What had happened was that Charlie had come home. He had walked up behind mother and playfully rubbed her legs like he was a cat. This scared mother, and with that, either Charlie or mother had to go. Mother won. I gave Charlie to a friend, who later said he had eaten all of his chickens. The last time that he had seen Charlie, he was back in the swamp running with a female red fox.

With my thoughts returning to the deer hunt, I turned off the dirt road and drove through the farmer's field, without waking the Smith's or their dogs. I stopped at the mud hold and stepped out of the truck. It was cold. The dead grass was white with frost. The water in the mud hole was frozen. I had my Carhartt overalls on over my blue jeans with a fleece-lined shirt. Putting the hunting coat on, I was on my way. Heading for the big oak, I slipped on the frozen ground. I quickly jumped up and looked around to see if anyone saw me. Then I smiled when I realized there wasn't anyone within half a mile from here. This time I walked slower to the big oak. It was time for a rest. I reached in the back of my hunting coat for a Wal-Mart grocery bag. I put it at the base of the tree to sit on. Wal-Mart bags have many uses.

Suddenly it came to me what I had done. I had left the 16 ga shells—from the squirrel hunt the day before—in the hunting coat. Now I had 16 ga shotgun shells and a 12 ga shotgun. That's an old folks' mistake that nobody had to know about, and I would never tell a soul. I would simply tell them, if I had to, that my gun wouldn't shoot. Better still, maybe the deer would go the other way. I sat down, disappointed at my blunder, but it was too late to go back now.

The morning air was very chilly. The wildlife was getting ready for the day. Birds were singing, and an old owl hooted. Behind me, I could hear the Smith's chickens waking up and crowing. It was 6:30 AM on the dot. I could hear the other hunters coming. The pickup trucks were bumping and spinning on the old-log road. The hunters stopped short of the clear-cut. They parked—all but Terry's truck. The hunters loaded into the back of Terry's four-wheel drive truck along with Terry's cur dog. Little John stayed so that he could turn John's walker dogs loose. About every seventy yards, Terry stopped to let a stander out of the truck. This happened all across the outer edge of the clear-cut. When the last man was out, Terry parked his truck and tooted his horn to let Little John know he was ready to start. I could hear chains rattling, tailgates opening, and dogs yelping. They were glad to get out of that bumpy truck.

Both drivers let out a yell. The hunt was on. Each driver was trying to scare the deer and to let the other hunters know where he was. This went on for a while. Out of the corner of my eye, I saw a movement. In front of my stand was a mound of dirt that the loggers had left. The movement came to the big mound of dirt. Stopping at the very top of the mound, the deer looked back at the drivers. That was when I saw him: Ol' Forked Horn. The sun was shining, yet the cold air made the vapor coming out of his nose and mouth look like smoke. Across the clear-cut, guns were shooting, dogs were barking, and drivers were yelling. This got the Smith's dogs upset, and they were barking. The walker dogs hit the big buck's trail and headed my way. Nearer they came.

At the bottom, deer were running everwhere. More guns sounded. Ol' Forked Horn had had enough. He headed straight for the big oak. He had not seen me yet. The muscles moving in his back and legs looked like a quarter horse. He came so close to me that he kicked frozen dirt onto my shoes. To this day, I do not know if I would have shot him anyway, even if I had the right shells. Why kill a legend?

The buck skidded to a stop when he saw my truck. I tried to jump up, but my leg was asleep. John's dogs were in front of me. I fell toward the dogs. It scared them so badly that they almost caught the deer. The Smiths' dogs had come out to meet the deer dogs. This boxed in the big buck. The only way to go was toward the farmhouses. Off he went between the two houses. The yard dogs and the deer dogs began to fight. The Smiths woke up, looked out of the window, and simultaneously saw the buck and dogs. It looked as if the buck had whipped both packs of dogs.

The fighting dogs had given the buck a chance to escape. I hobbled to my truck and turned onto the dirt road to try to catch the dogs. After catching all the deer dogs and tying them in the back of my truck, I headed for the store. I knew that the other hunters would soon be coming out as well. I had barely gotten into the store when the other hunters came. They were glad to see that I had their dogs. They drank Mountain Dews and Big Oranges and ate every nick-knack that Sam had. Right away, we started planning another hunt. Terry had picked out a good place.

Just then, a man in an old car drove in. "Why don't you go after Ol' Forked Horn?" he said. "He is standing in Frank's field, now." John grabbed the dogs, and we headed for Frank's field. We wanted to run the big, blue buck again, so we put standers along Bee Creek, southwest of Frank's field. But this time, the Forked Horn ran north until he crossed the main road. That's where the dogs lost his trail. So we caught the dogs and went back to the store to swap tales of the morning hunt. Everyone was excited, especially because doe season was in. Today they had killed six deer. Two were bucks and four doe. I say "they," because I still had my little secret about the shotgun shells.

One man from our group said that he had seen a deer coming. He said, "I shot at him and missed. I shot at him again and hit him in the same place. The faster he ran, the farther he went. The farther he went, the faster he ran. The last time I saw him, he was out of sight." Another man said he shot three times at a deer, but when Terry ran it down, there were no bullet holes in it. The Jones brothers were standing next to each other when one shot down a deer. The younger brother came to help. The deer was trying to get away. The older brother said, "Hold its leg. If it kicks you, it won't hurt." The younger brother said, "It was kicking down pine saplings; won't hurt nothing."

The hunters decided to go and dress the deer and make another hunt in the afternoon. I said, "No, thank you; maybe next year."

While we were talking, Po Boy had ridden his mule to the gristmill with his shelled corn in a sack, tied behind his saddle. He untied his corn and took it to the gristmill shed. Po Boy went back and tied his mule with a longer rope, and I walked back to the gristmill with him.

Meanwhile, Ol' Forked Horn had made his way along the fencerow, almost to where the mule was tied. About this time, the mail carrier pulled up to the store's mailbox. He ran over a sharp rock that blew out a tire. The mule's rope had looped around his back leg. When the tire blew out, it scared the mule. He jumped, and the tangled rope threw the mule down. Now on the other side of the fence was Ol' Forked Horn. The noise made him jump the fence where the fallen mule was. We ran to the door of the gristmill just in time to see the deer and mule getting up. Sam said that the buck had knocked the mule down. The scared mule broke the rope, and he and the big buck were off to the races. The mule's saddle horn caught the clothesline where two white towels were hanging. When the line broke, the towels sailed into the air and one towel got caught on Forked Horns antler. Big Sam's wife, looking out the window, saw the towel going into the bushes and started yelling for Sam to call the law. Someone had stolen her towels and had run into the bushes. I laughed so much that my sides were hurting.

I paid Big Sam for the fresh corn meal and started for my truck. I was thinking, *What else could happen in one day?* Just then, an old man drove up. He said that he might need something a little stronger than Coca Cola because he could swear he had just seen Ol' Forked Horn taking a bath in the creek. He said that the buck even had a white towel to use to dry off. Big Sam said, "You haven't seen nothing; we just saw him knock Po Boy's mule over."

The Christmas Wishes

Word had gotten out about the big, bad buck. It seemed as if every hunter in Alabama was trying to be the one to kill that Ol' Forked Horn. We tried the next year. After he outsmarted us one time, we planned a hunt; but it rained us out. There was nothing for us to do but wait for the next season.

Now that summer had finally ended, the weather was getting a bit cooler, and the leaves had started changing colors. Hunters started getting *hunting fever*. My mind filled with plans to outsmart Ol' Forked Horn this year.

I went to town to get a new supply of buckshot, but on my way home, I decided to take a different route past the low-rent apartments. There was Jim Smith sitting under a big, water oak tree. He did not look up. He seemed to be looking off into space. I stopped and got out to talk with him. I thought maybe he was visiting someone here, but he looked at me and said, "You don't know? Ol' Forked Horn's tales ran me out of my home." He said that the Forked Horn tales had brought those night hunters. "They had four-wheel drive pickup trucks with big spotlights. They came at all times of the night. They shot our dogs and threw beer cans all over the old-log road. Then one night, they killed both of our mules."

Jim said "The mule killing upset John Henry so much that he had a heart attack. That's what the doctor had said after John Henry passed away. With John Henry gone, it just wasn't the same. John Henry's wife went to live with her children somewhere up north. I didn't have a mule or money to buy another one. I probably couldn't have found one, anyway. A mule is as hard to find as hen's teeth, so I brought my woman here to live.

Jim continued, "This ain't no life for me. Nothing to do but sit all day. It ain't no wonder the young folks take drugs. They are trying to pass the day. What they need is work. I wish someone would hire me. They think that I am too old. I would almost work for free. I have worked all my life. In a way, that Ol' Forked Horn took my brother John Henry and took my way of life. Why don't one of y'all kill him? I know it is hard to do, but I can show you where you can box him in. You see, with no crops to eat, he will move over the ridge to a hardwood slue." I told Jim "OK," and we planned to go next Tuesday.

I picked up Jim on Tuesday and we headed to the old-home place. Jim wouldn't stop talking—until we go to the old, dirt road. I stopped at the cold spring to get a drink. As I looked over at Jim, his head was down. I thought that I saw a tear in his eyes. After getting my water, I stayed a little longer. I wanted to give Jim some time with his thoughts.

After we started on, Jim said, "Stop at the south-field road." He thought that I knew where that was—but I didn't—so I just said, "Say when." Soon he said when. We turned off the road, and he said we could drive through the field, which was now just a weed patch.

We had driven a short way when Jim said that we had better stop here. When we got out of the pickup, Jim led the way. We passed ten or twelve old, fifty-five gallon drums. I said, "Somebody must have had an oil well here." And Jim replied with a grin, "It was an oil well, alright."

We worked our way over a hill—though it seemed more like a mountain. Jim pointed to the water oak trees: "You see," he said, "there are not a whole lot of folks who know about this place." He said that all this land had been in their family for a long time, but that there are so many Ayres that it is not worth much to any one of them. He added, "This place kept us fed with squirrel, coon, rabbits, and sometimes a deer. We grew all of our other food. With the profits we got from the 'oil well' and the eggs that we sold, we had enough money to buy flour and a few clothes." He looked straight at me and said, "Mister, that was a good life. Not like where we live now, pinned up like a fatting hog." Jim told me that he had always looked after the land. He said, "Ya'll can hunt on it at any time." (I knew that by "ya'll" he meant the local hunters and me.)

As we started back to the truck, we spooked a rabbit. It headed toward the old fields. "That him," Jim said. I looked over at Jim and said, "Him, who?"

He had a smile on his face and said, "That was no rabbit. That was John Henry. I am glad that he made it back. I hope when I die, I will come back as a rabbit, also." I looked at Jim and asked him if he wasn't a rabbit, what would he be, and he said, "probably a snake." I tried to tell him that the Bible tells us that if we accept Christ and are born again, we would go to live with Jesus when we die. If we don't accept Christ as our Savior, then we will go to hell when we die. There was nothing about coming back as a rabbit.

When we got to the truck, we headed back to Jim's new home, and Jim said if we ever kill Ol' Forked Horn, he would sure like to see him. It was at that moment that a big buck jumped into the road. Jim yelled, "That's him, that's Ol' Forked Horn!" The deer had at least a ten-point rack. I wanted to know why he thought that this deer was Ol' Forked Horn, and Jim said, "Didn't you see that white streak on his left-front leg?" Then I remembered that day at the big oak when he ran past me. I sure had seen the white streak on his leg.

Jim said the buck had cut his leg when he was young and had gotten tangled up in barbed wire: "Me and John Henry tried to kill him with bean sticks. He got away with his cut leg and that is probably why he hates us so much today."

The week before dog-hunting season, I scouted out a new hunting place and saw just a few deer tracks. When the farmer left, I guess the deer left, too. Both were hunting for food.

I called Terry and told him what I had found. He asked if the tracks of the big buck were there. I told him that one set of tracks was as big as a young calf. I had said enough. We had to try Ol' Forked Horn again, and so we started planning the hunt. We could put standers on the dirt road and by the old house. We could get Harry, R.D., and Tater Bug to come in the back way, and they could stand on the King Family's land.

The hunt was planned for a time when everyone would be off work. We decided that December 24 would be the day of the big hunt. At sunrise, we would all start for our places. Terry had gotten Cecil to go with him. I called Joe Bill to meet me at the store, and we went to the place where Jim had taken me.

Now, going up that steep hill on frozen grass took about all the energy we could muster. We got to a rocky place, and Joe Bill slipped down. His gun hit one of those rocks, and it broke in two. He would not be able to shoot it, but being a good guy, he went on with me. Maybe he could help me drag the deer back if I killed one.

When we got to the top of the hill and looked out across the oak slue, there was so much white frost that it looked as if it had snowed. The stillness of the morning was worth the climb. We felt anything but cold. That didn't last long, and soon the chill began to sink in.

Terry turned his cur dogs loose, and he let out a yell. John had come in by the graveyard road and turned his walkers loose. His dogs struck a fresh track. We could hear them yelping and barking.

Terry's dogs had jumped a deer. It ran toward Terry, and he killed it with one shot. By now, John's walkers were in the middle of the oak thicket. You could tell by the sound of their barks that they had jumped a deer, and they were heading my way. They turned back and were headed toward the King place. You would think that they had killed a truckload from all the shooting. After all of that shooting, we only two deer to show for it.

The walker dogs headed back toward Terry, and that is when they spooked the big buck. He headed for the old house place. Then he saw one of the standers move. It was so cold, and the stander had started to move around to keep warm. This movement caused Ol' Forked Horn to start back to where he had come from. That is when Joe Bill saw the big buck and tried to tell me without spooking the deer again. The big buck jumped the road so close to Joe Bill that he could have hit him with a spitball.

Ol' Forked Horn ran at least one hundred yards from me, and I fired two shots at him. He ran into the oak slue. One driver took a long shot at him. This turned the old buck. This time he made a beeline for the spring crossing and crossed the road, unseen by the young hunter. When the dogs crossed the road, the stander said that they must have been running after a ghost. The deer tracks prove different.

As Terry was heading back to his truck, he jumped a spike buck, and Cecil killed it.

Two deer were killed on the King place. Terry killed one, and Cecil killed the other. We had killed four deer in all. It was not a bad morning hunt. The negative thing was that we had let Ol' Forked Horn get the best of us, again.

We caught what dogs we could and headed for Big Sam's store. There sat an eighteen-wheeler. Something had knocked the hood off and bent the fender. The driver of the eighteen-wheeler said that a very big deer had jumped in front of him and he had hit him. His truck and trailer wheels had run over the deer. It had to be Ol' Forked Horn. His antlers were broken off.

I had to know, so I headed to the spot where he had hit the deer. It was a bloody mess with hair, bones, and guts everywhere.

The body looked like hamburger meat. I looked for the left-front leg and saw that it was brown all over. I was relieved to find that the leg had no white in sight. Now, although some believed that the legend had been killed that day, I knew better—there would be another hunt. Of course, if this had happened a year ago, the Smiths would still be happy farming and moonshining, "oil welling, that is."

Before going to dress the deer we had killed, R D asked Harry what he wanted for Christmas, and he replied, "More buckshot." Joe Bill wanted his shotgun repaired. They asked me, and after thinking for a while, I smiled and said, "Maybe a Forked Horn, Jr."

Forked Horn, Jr.

Christmas was over, and we were off to hunt Forked Horn, Jr. He proved to be as smart as his dad— dodging standers and tree stands, eating at night, hiding by day. He was so good that some said it was not Junior at all. It was Forked Horn's spirit. They say that man or truck cannot kill spirits.

The last day of hunting season, we planned to hunt for this so-called Junior. We put standers at the same place as before. Bunk had stopped at the end stand, near the road. All at once, the dogs jumped a herd of deer. Deer were running everywhere. Guns were shooting, and drovers were yelling. We heard Bunk shoot and thought he had killed a doe. When we got to him, there lay a big buck with a large set of antlers. This deer probably weighed one hundred seventy pounds.

We took Bunk's deer to the store because that was the designated gathering place. It seemed as if every bunch of standers had killed between one and three deer.

An old, black man was looking at Bunk's deer with its big set of antlers, and someone asked what he thought it would weigh. He ran his hand along its back, then he looked again at the big rack. He said it would go between six hundred fifty and seven hundred pounds. I thought, *If a man could be fooled this badly, even after rubbing a deer with a rack like that, it is no wonder people get buck fever.*

On my way home, I went by the apartment to see Jim and to tell him about the seven hundred pound deer. Jim said, "That was a big one." Then he looked me in the eyes and asked, "What about Ol' Forked Horn? Now, tell me the truth."

I smiled and said, "He's alive and doing well."

"That's all I wanted to hear," said Jim. "I hate him, but as long as he runs free, John Henry will hop around and keep his eyes on him." Jim asked about the deer that the trucker had run over, and I told him that there wasn't any white streak on its leg.

"Only you and I know about that," I said. "Just wait until next year, we will hunt him again.

The Big Fire

The summer had been a long, hot one. It hadn't rained for the last three months. It was dryer than I had ever seen, and most of the creeks had stopped running. Even the ponds had dried up. It had to rain before the state would open deer season.

The last week of September, it started to cloud up. We were hoping for rain, and when it came, lightning was streaking down everywhere. That is when it happened. The lightning struck a tree near the old Stave Mill houses. The dry grass and weeds started to burn. The wind was blowing hard, and this made the fire spread faster. It burned across the old fields and caught the old houses ablaze. They went up in a smoke.

The fire burned from the creek bank to the blacktop road. What had happened to the wildlife? Had Ol' Forked Horn gotten trapped? I wanted to know, so I loaded up in my old pickup truck and headed out to investigate.

When I got to the dirt road, it was an awful sight. Acre after acre was now a sea of black. The cold-water spring was still running. I passed the spring and stopped at the south field. Fire had burned the old field. I thought about Jim saying that the rabbit was his brother, John Henry. Then the thought entered my mind, *If the rabbit was dead, what would Jim think it would come back as?*

Slowly I climbed to the top of the big hill. The fire had not crossed over to the oak slue. Had Forked Horn actually made it out? As I walked on toward the oaks, a rabbit jumped up and ran into the thicket. I wasn't looking for rabbit. I had Forked Horn on my mind. As I walked on, there were more fifty-five gallon drums. You could see where there had been several fires. This was where the moon shiner's distillery or oil well—or whatever you want to call it—had been. I will just call it the Smith's oil wells. By the look of the old fire signs, it had been at least five years since anyone had used it.

The springs that fed the slue had water in them. I slipped along the banks until I spotted a large deer standing in the shallow water. The buck had a big rack. Ragged skin covered his antlers; he was losing his velvet. He had grown a new set of antlers through the summer. Now in the next few weeks, he would rub off that old skin, leaving the new, polished rack. This takes place every year.

The burned dust had gotten into my nose, and I had to sneeze. Of course, this alerted the deer, and he came out of the water in a flash. As he turned to the left, I saw it: the white stripe on his leg. It was Ol' Forked Horn.

When I got home, I had to tell the guys. This let the cat out of the bag. I had to tell them about the white markings on his leg. Then I told them that Junior never existed. It was Forked Horn all the time. I had kept my mouth shut so that the pressure would not be on Forked Horn.

When the rains had started, there was water everywhere. The grass and weeds started growing again. By deer season, the old Smith Farm looked almost the same, except that the houses were gone.

By Halloween, we had already planned a way to stop the big buck—but I guess he had a plan of his own.

The first day of dog-hunting season, we were ready. We jumped several deer and killed some. Still no Forked Horn. I wondered if someone else had killed him or if he had moved away.

The day after our big hunt, I went by and picked up Jim. We headed for the old-home place. Jim was as talkative as ever. When we got to the burned-down houses, Jim said that he had many good times while living there. He said that there were times when he thought he might freeze to death in the winter or burn up in the summer, but that the one good thing was that they were never hungry.

As we got out and walked to where the old houses had been, we were looking for tracks. The ashes had made the weeds grow. Over by the old hog pen was a tall, thick bunch of weeds. As we walked toward them, a deer that looked as big as a mule jumped up. He headed for the oak slue. When he got out of the tall weeds, we could see that he had a white stripe on his leg.

I could not wait to tell the other hunters. We had to change our plans now. We had to hunt the fields instead of the oak slue. We began to make our plans. The next Saturday's hunt was on.

However, we got a late start. When we got to the fields, a bird hunter had already jumped Ol' Forked Horn. The bird hunter said that he could not help himself. He shot a big, big buck in the rear end with his birdshots, and then he pointed and said, "He went that way."

This ended our hunt in this area, and we headed for another location. After that, we often called Ol' Forked Horn the Old Sore Tail.

This was the fourth year that Old Sore Tail had outsmarted us—but we had another plan.

Never Give Up

The next week, I went to Big Sam's store. The tales had gotten bigger and bigger. Now Forked Horn was a ghost that could fly. He even went in houses and took people's money. People blamed him for every car wreck within twenty miles.

I said that we would have his horns and nail them on Big Sam's gristmill wall. That was when someone said that Ol' Forked Horn had burned the Smith's fields and that the gristmill would burn if we nailed the deer's horns there.

The next Saturday, we all got up early for the hunt. Today was the day for Mr. Sore Tail. We put our standers along the road and down by the cold-water spring. Terry's cur dogs jumped first. The deer headed away from the standers. Terry was running, trying to cut off the deer when he slipped down. When Terry fell, his gun barrel filled with mud. He grabbed a big weed and punched out the mud, but in his hurry to reload, he put in a chap stick instead of a shell.

The buck was coming. Terry tried to shoot, but the gun snapped. The chap stick just would not shoot.

However, he did manage to turn the buck toward the cold-water spring.

When we put the standers out, an old man and his grandson took the stand by the spring. The old man had a 12 ga shotgun. The boy had a 410, loaded with birdshot. When the old man saw the deer with such a huge rack, in his excitement, he shot two times in the dirt. The boy kept his cool. When the buck passed by, the boy shot him in the rear, thus keeping Ol' Sore Tail's tail sore.

The big, blue buck had outsmarted us again. Just wait until the next hunt. We will get him.

True to our word, we hunted for Ol' Forked Horn again, but still had no luck. Even his tracks were gone. Could it be possible that he was dead? I scouted the field and slue repeatedly, but there was not a track or any sign of him.. *That was it!* They had put out more corn than Big Sam could grind in two days. Moreover, Ol' Forked Horn had found it and was staying near it. He was too sly to come out in the daylight, so he was eating the corn at night.

After that, most of our hunters started hunting in other places, but not me. I checked the area regularly, but had no luck finding the big deer. It

Then one day when I stopped by Big Sam's store, I heard that the Big Hill Hunting Club members had seen deer tracks big enough to frame was the middle of January, and I was about to give up when I decided to give it one more try. I figured rutting season would bring him out, and it did. I spotted his large tracks and could tell he had followed a smaller set of tracks. I was almost back to my truck when I spotted a doe and a big, slick buck. The corn had made Ol' Forked Horn fat and sassy, and he was looking good. Unfortunately, dog-hunting season was over, and that meant the season was over for this hunter.

I don't see any sport in sitting in a dry-shooting house over a green patch, with corn and apples to bait the deer. I figured these hunters spend enough money on shooting houses, deer feed, and permits that they could buy a fat steer, climb up a tree, and shoot. The beef would taste better than venison, anyway. Most of the time, they only take part of the deer and leave the rest in the field to rot.

Another summer had come and gone. Now it was late August, and I had started scouting for deer signs again. We had had some strong winds, and when I got to the oak slue, I found many oak trees blown down. I was having trouble getting through when I spotted a deer tangled in the fallen trees. It looked as if an oak had fallen on it. The deer was still alive but in poor condition. He had been there for over a week without food or water because the tree limbs had him pinned down.

I had to make the long journey back over the hill to go to my truck and get an ax. After getting the ax and hiking back over the hill to where the deer was stuck, I was just as out of breath as the deer and needed a short rest before trying to free him. I began to cut away tree limb after tree limb in order to free him. It would have been good if my ax had been sharper. The deer looked so weak and helpless. I felt sorry for him as I started to help him up. Getting to his feet, he turned toward me, and I thought he wanted to thank me. Wrong! He charged toward me. It was a weak charge. I had my ax and could have hit him with it, but instead, I just backed up into the tops and quickly got out of his way. As he passed by me, I saw it: the white stripe on his front leg.

I stayed in the treetops until Mr. Forked Horn headed for some water. His antlers were in velvet and still soft. The fallen tree limbs had knocked his antlers downward, and they were bruised and bleeding. I felt sorry for him. Now, he was injured and had a lot of healing to do if he lived. In this condition, a coyote could kill him. However, it was possible that nothing would spot him.

I had to take the long climb over the hill to my truck. As I was going over the hill, I wondered how many times the Smith brothers had packed their "oil well" products over this same hill.

It was late when I arrived home. As I sat down to enjoy a good, hot meal, I wondered how Ol' Forked Horn was and if he would live. I decided to give him two weeks to recover before trying to find him again.

True to my promise, two weeks later, I returned to the Smith's place. Looking toward the junkyard pool, I could see buzzards flying around. This almost broke my heart.

The first time that I had seen Ol' Forked Horn was at this very place. Was it going to be the last? It had to be him. I turned to start back home but just could not make myself leave. I had to see for myself.

After parking the truck, I started walking toward the big oak. The stink in the air was bad. Looking, but not really wanting to see, I walked on toward where the buzzards were. One flew up. There, lying in the road, was a dead snake. I danced a little jig of joy. It looked as if a deer had stomped the snake to death. Walking on, I could see that the big oak was loaded with young, green acorns. There were plenty of deer tracks, and one set was as big as a calf's track. This had to be my buck. There was a little more spring in my step as I started back to my truck.

The walk had made me a bit thirsty, and when I got to the cold-water spring, I stopped for a drink. That is when I caught sight of a skinny deer with a dropped set of antlers.

He was off in a flash, but before he was out of sight, I spotted his identifying, white-striped leg. He was alive! I said aloud, *"Just you wait till next season, old buddy; we will meet again."*

Hunting Is Good for You

Deer season was drawing near, and I had already gotten the fever—deer hunting fever, that is.

I got up early one morning and went by Jim's apartment to get him to go with me. There was a young man there who said, "Jim don't stay here no more, he done moved."

Disappointed, I left and decided to check out the fields by myself. I turned onto the old dirt road, and to my surprise, the county had graded the road. There was a new power line running along the side of the road. I drove on to the cold-water spring, and there sat a mobile home. I stopped my truck and got out as a man came out of the front door of the home. I could not believe my eyes. It was Jim himself, all smiles. I asked Jim when he had moved. As I stood there, listening to Jim, he told me about his two sons. They had bought the trailer for him. He told me they had dug out the spring and put an electric well pump in it. They had also put in the septic tank. "I am home now. I have seen John Henry lots of times. Po Boy said he felt as if he was too old to farm any more, and so he sold me his mule. I have done bought my seeds, and I can hardly wait until spring to start putting them in the ground. My woman is happy here. If you see anybody with chickens for sell, let me know."

Jim asked how I had been doing and said he knew what I was doing there. He said, "He still here. I saw him the other day, up close. His head is starting to grey like mine, but he still up to any chase ya'll can give him."

Jim was right; he did know what I was doing there. We both climbed into my truck, and we headed to the south field. Jim had knocked down all the weeds, and we started looking for deer signs. There were plenty of tracks. I just nodded to Jim.

We would be back to try again if it was all right with him. Jim said, "You know it is. When ya'll hunt, I will take the stand by my trailer home."

As we started back, Jim asked if I would take him to Big Sam's store, and I did. In the store, there were three men sitting and sharing their stories. They were glad to see Jim.

Jim bought a few things and was still in the store as I listened to the latest on Ol' Forked Horn. One man said that he had seen him fly across the road. Another said that he had wrecked two more trucks; and one man—whom I had never seen—said that Ol' Forked Horn had knocked down a tree that nearly killed him. It had made him so mad that he knocked off every limb on the tree. That was what made his horns droop.

When Jim came out of the store, he had a paper bag and a crockery sack. Big Sam's wife had given Jim a cat, and had put it in the crockery sack. Now the ride in the pickup had upset that cat, and it started howling. Just as we reached the dirt road, the cat got out of the bag and started to climb my arm. Jim grabbed it by the tail. The harder he pulled, the harder the cat dug in. I was swerving all over the road. When Jim finally pulled the cat off of me, the claws ripped my arm, and blood was running down my arm. I managed to get the truck stopped. By then the cat had bitten Jim. That was one mad cat. Jim opened the door, and the cat jumped out. As he ran through the straw patch, a rabbit jumped up and ran straight toward Jim. By now, Jim was out of the truck and laughing: "John Henry never did like cats," he said.

I washed my arm in the cold water from the spring and left, but not before telling Jim that we would be back to try again.

We planned our next hunt for the following Saturday. We would have the drivers turn the dogs loose in the south field. We would stand the Ridge road and the King place. John would put some of his standers on the graveyard road, but the weather turned bad as soon as we started our hunt. Just as the dogs jumped, it started to rain, and the standers headed for cover.

Terry stopped his dogs. John's walkers were fresh, and on they went. Forked Horn ran the road on the King place. No shots were fired. Then he ran the Graveyard Road. One man with a rain suit tried to shoot, but the blinding rain made him miss. The shot made the deer turn, and he ran the ridge road. Again, no shots were fired. The dogs followed the buck through the fields and back into the slue. By now, Mr. Forked Horn had a good lead on the hounds, and it was not long until the rain had washed away any scent of a deer. Eventually, the rain stopped, and the sun came out. With Terry and his cur dogs, we managed to kill a couple of deer. However, the big, bad, blue buck would live another day.

After that, we went after Ol' Forked Horn several more times but did not jump him any more that season. In the fall, the leaves started to change color. Even though I had given up on deer hunting by that time of the year, I would still get restless. One season was all I could bear to skip hunting, and the next season as the leaves began to change, I said to myself, *Why don't you go hunting? It is good for your health. The walking and the fresh air will make you feel good.*

I called the hunters to see if they wanted to go. They had a club down by the river bottom, and they asked me to go with them, but I said "No thanks."

Not wanting to be outdone, I got up early the next morning and went to the Smith place. I parked at the large mud hole and walked past the big oak tree until the road started to go into the bottomland. There was a wide ditch in front of me with a game trail along side of it. I needed the rest, and I sat down by an old, burned tree stump. I must have sat there for half an hour or more. I could hear dogs running and heading my way. They were getting closer by the minute, and I could hear the deer jumping through the weeds. He ran the game trail along the big ditch. Just before he reached the road, he stopped and looked back at the oncoming dogs.

I thought back. This was what Ol' Forked Horn had done. Could it be some of his offsprings? I raised my gun. Why kill him? Just watching him was enough. He bounced out of the path and onto the road. He was running within fifteen feet of me. I watched as his feet hit the road with ease. Then he sprung up again. This deer was smaller than Ol' Forked Horn. I watched the dogs come out of the weeds and run up the game trail, then onto the road. Listening to the dogs, I knew that the deer had seen my truck and had turned to the south where there were a few houses.

I could hear the yard dogs barking at the deer dogs. A few minutes later, it was calm again. The birds started singing again. I ate the apple that I had packed in my hunting coat, and when I got to the old oak tree, I could hear the deer dogs coming back. I sat down and waited to see which way the dogs would come from. They were running the same route, only in reverse. The deer ran past me a second time, and still I did not shoot. I did say, "Three times and you are out." The dogs had to be at least a mile behind him this time.

As I pulled out and headed home, I was thinking that I would hang up my gun. When I got to Jim's mobile home, he was standing outside with his shotgun. He said that he could hear the deer dogs earlier and that he had seen a big set of deer tracks in his new field. Jim said, "Let me show you. We went to Jim's field and sure enough, there they were. A set of tracks as big a young calf's tracks. It had to be Ol' Forked Horn. No other deer had tracks that big, and Jim said that he had not seen them until last week.

It just didn't take much to trigger that deer-hunting fever, and right then and there, a deer hunt started clicking in my ear. It looks as if this gun will stay out of retirement a little longer.

I called the hunters to tell them about finding the big tracks. They already had a hunt planned but agreed to try later. We made several hunts, and even though I had seen the tracks, we did not jump him once.

Jim gave me word to come to his place, so on a Monday after a wet weekend, I drove there. He met me with a puzzled look on his face, and when I asked him what the matter was, he said that Ol' Forked Horn had turned into a Mrs. Forked Horns. He said that he had seen the big deer several times and it even had a white stripe on its front leg. I did not know what to tell him, but on my way home, I stopped by Big Sam's store where I heard that several times, a doe had been seen. She was as big as Ol' Forked Horn. They said that she must have weighed over two hundred pounds. Now, that is a big doe, so I put my binoculars in the pickup.

It rained most of the following week, and I and had gotten cabin fever trying to sit and wait for the rain to stop. Finally, it stopped raining, and I started for Jim's field. When I got to the south field, there was Jim, walking and looking in the road for tracks. I stopped, and Jim got into my pickup. We drove to the old-home place. We were still sitting in the truck talking when a big deer entered the field. I got out my binoculars. I could not see any antlers. What I did see was the white stripe on its front leg. It was our big doe, and on my way home, I started thinking about her. I wanted to see a doe that old buck, and when it turned its head, I could see what looked like big buttons on its head. His face was almost white now. I guess he was too old to grow antlers anymore.

Now, the word got around about the huge doe, and hunters were trying to kill the trophy deer. Jim said "They don started to night hunt again.". He wondered what he was going to do. He sure didn't want to loose another mule. I told him that the best thing to do was to put up a gate near the paved road and post his land. That might stop them—that is, if they didn't knock down the gate.

Jim put up a strong gate and posted his land. He said, "You know that this don't mean ya'll." I thanked him and then said, "Since the big buck doesn't have antlers, we probably won't be back." It had always been a challenge, but who would want to kill an old, gray-headed deer. The meat would be so tough that you could not even stick a fork in the gravy.

The Big Buck Returns

The following fall, I saw Jim at Wal-Mart. He said, "Keep this under your hat: Ol' Forked Horn is back and is as fat as ever. He should be. He's been trying to eat everything that I had planted." He continued, "Back in the early summer, I took a shot at him. He is not so tame now. It is hard to get a good look at him, but I did see that fat rascal jumping into the thicket a couple of times. Ya'll need to try him one more time. If you do, you will need these." He gave me the key to the gate and said that the gate had stopped the night hunting.

It was the week before Christmas, and I went and scouted out the fields and the oak slue. There were big tracks in both places.

With Jim working the fields almost everyday, I figured Ol' Forked Horn would probably bed down in the thickets around the oak slue, so I got up with our hunters to plan one more hunt. Our plan was to turn the dogs loose on the King place. We would stand the graveyard road and the ridge road. I always stood on the ridge road. From there, I could hear the dogs.

I enjoy listening to the dogs running. They seemed to be calling to the other dogs to tell them they had found the fresh track; they were saying "catch me if you can."

The day we had chosen to hunt for the old, blue buck was bad. The wind had started blowing in a cold front. Deer know how to pick a bedding place on the south side of a hill so that the north wind will not hit them. Our drivers know this, also.

With the standers in place, the drivers started the hunt, hooting and hollering on the south side of the hills. The dogs struck a fresh track, and I could hear the cur dog's fine voices and the walker dog's deep, base voices.

Now, on windy days, deer will run with their noses in the wind; this proved to be true this day. The men on the graveyard road were in the right place. The problem was that they could not hear the dogs. The deer would be jumping the road before the standers were ready. This happened two or three times, and the deer would be gone by the time the standers heard them. From where I stood, I could see the oak slue, and it had an opening where the storm had blown down the oaks.

Jim had cut firewood from the fallen oaks. He did not have a fireplace in his trailer home, so he sold the firewood. He probably used the limbs to fire up his *oil wells*. Anyway, the storm had left a good opening through the slue.

I soon saw a fox trot through the opening. The dogs had spooked the fox. Shortly after that, I spotted a large deer slipping along the slue. At some point, it would wade into the water. The dogs had not picked up his trail yet, and the path that he was taking would miss all of our standers.

I started running—if you could call it running—trying to cut off the deer. I would run a short distance and stop to see where he was. I was breathing so hard and my heart was beating so fast that I soon gave up and sat down to rest. By now, the dogs had hit his trail. I saw the dogs taking the same path that the deer had taken earlier. They were having a hard time following the deer after it had walked in the water, but they soon figured it out.

Soon the deer and the dogs were out of my sight. They had gone in a thicket near the bottom of the ridge road where I was. The big deer turned back along a game trail at the foot of the ridge. This would put the deer in a position to cross the ridge road where I had been.

I was winded and couldn't run anymore, so I stood on a large rock that enabled me to see him as he crossed the road. He crossed in a single leap. In that split second, I was able to see the white stripe on its front leg and a head full of antlers. The dogs crossed a few minutes later and were soon gone from my range of hearing. He had outsmarted us again.

After I caught my breath, I started back to my truck. When I reached the truck, there stood Jim. He had caught most of the dogs. We tied them in the back of my truck and Jim said that he had seen John Henry running out of the weed patch when the dogs came through.

Ol' Forked Horn must have been a long ways ahead of the dogs because Jim had not seen him. I told him that it was Ol' Forked Horn alright. I had seen the white-striped leg.

Jim told me to come back to his trailer after I took the dogs to the drovers and he would give me some of the best sweet taters I ever had.

When I got to the gate, there were the rest of the hunters. They loaded up their dogs and headed for Big Sam's store, and I went back to Jim's where he gave me some red sweet potatoes.

Heading home, I saw the other hunters at Big Sam's store. They were loading up to make another drive, but I told them "No, thank you." I did not want to go on another hunt today.

As I started to leave the store, a commercial fisherman stopped me. He asked me if we were hunting this morning. I just nodded and asked why. He said that when he was loading his boat onto his trailer, he had seen the biggest buck deer that he had ever seen. It was swimming the river. He had a grey head, and his leg was white striped. "When I got the boat loaded," he said, "Two walker dogs jumped into the back of my pickup. They wanted a ride; the only thing was, a ride to where?"

I knew they were John's dogs, and so I put them in my truck. I could not find the other hunters so I just took the dogs to John's dog pen.

As I was driving home, I started thinking about the last time I had seen Ol' Forked Horn, before today. He was down and out. I thought his days were numbered.

Today, however, he had outsmarted the hunters and their dogs, again.

He was a legendary deer. He will probably die of old age. He is too smart for us to kill, and I am glad that we didn't. I really do not think that Jim wanted him dead, either. He just wanted him gone.

I guess it was an obsession with me to try to outsmart Ol' Forked Horn, and he had me hooked.

The rest of our group was hunting at the River Bottom Club. I could not stay at home, but I did not want to hunt the river bottom.

One warm morning (if you can call fifty degrees "warm"), I got my old, double barrel and headed to Big Sam's store. I wanted the latest information on Ol' Forked Horn. Word was out that nearly every day he had been seen down by the west side of the river. There must have been plenty of acorns there for him to feed on.

As I was about to leave, the fisherman stopped. He was the same man that had brought John's dogs to me the other day. I asked him about the big buck, and he said that he had seen him several times. He said that whenever he came into the boat landing, he had seen the buck swimming to the east side of the river. The fisherman shook his head, saying, "That's a big buck."

I went by Jim's, and his wife told me that Jim was helping his friend kill hogs. I asked her to tell Jim that Ol' Forked Horn is on his way back, and that the fisherman had seen him swimming the river today.

On my way home, I met Jim walking. He was leading a red-bone hound dog. I stopped to chat for a minute. Jim was proud of his dog. He said that he was going to call him Old Red. Looking over toward me, he said, "Why don't you come back tomorrow and we can try him out." I just nodded.

The next day was beautiful, and when I got to Jim's around seven AM, he had Old Red tied on a rope lease. We walked up the hill behind Jim's trailer. I turned right to get on the ridge road that overlooked the oak slue. Jim took Old Red down in the lower slue bottom and turned him loose. In no time at all, Old Red let out with a long-sounding bark. Then he started with a short-chop bark. I knew what had happened. He had treed a squirrel. Jim started shooting. He shot five times, and I suppose he killed the squirrel because Old Red stopped barking. On they went, repeating this over and over. Meanwhile, I was watching the opening in the oak slue. Old Red treed again. Jim shot. This was too much for whatever was in the slue, and as he started slipping out, I could see that it was our blue buck. He went into the thicket at the base of the ridge where I was. I waited a couple of minutes and saw him coming back on the game trail.

This time, I knew where he would cross the ridge road. I got to the spot, hiding behind a spicewood bush. I didn't have to wait long. Here he came, stopping at the edge of the road. He looked back toward Jim and his dog. When the buck moved, instead of jumping the road, he just stepped out. That white stripe was shining in the sunlight. He was less than twelve feet from me. I checked his rack, and he was at least a nine point.

I did not even raise my gun. I just stepped out from behind the spicewood bush and pointed my finger at him as I said aloud, "Bang! Bang!" Ol' Forked Horn coiled up like a slinky and jumped a small-pine sapling. There was the sound of intense grunting and bushes shaking, and then he was gone.

I sat there on a big rock and waited for Jim. When Jim got to me, he was grinning as he showed me his squirrels.

Old Red sniffed the bushes and the tracks where Ol' Forked Horn had gone earlier. He did not even try to run the deer. He just stood there with his bristles raised.

I told Jim that Ol' Forked Horn must have outwitted us again. Jim didn't care. He had himself a fine squirrel dog.

I went home to retire my old, double-barrel gun, knowing that today I could have, but didn't. Although the big buck is getting old now, he had given us eight seasons of the greatest hunting any hunter could ask for.

Jim and His Shadow

Big Red was the best thing that could have happened to Jim. When Jim went to his fields, Big Red went with him. While Jim worked, Big Red hunted—treeing squirrels, digging out field mice, and sometimes running rabbits.

Now, running a rabbit was a "no-no" according to Jim. Jim would scold Red for running rabbits and tell him that it might be John Henry.

With all the barking that Big Red did and with Jim being in the fields, the deer moved over to the oak slue.

When the leaves started turning color, I went to see Jim. He had raised a good crop of corn and sweet potatoes. Jim said that he even raised a few peas. He said that Big Red was like his shadow and that he couldn't make a move without Red following him. He told me that Big Red had treed him a coon. I looked toward the big oak, and that was when Jim said he had not seen him or his tracks. I knew whom he was talking about. Big Red had kept the deer away.

On my way home, I stopped at Big Sam's store. Nobody had seen Ol' Forked Horn. Big Sam's wife wanted to give me a cat. I thanked her and said that the last cat she gave anybody almost scratched off my arm. She just laughed and said that this was the same cat. She said, "It just keeps coming back."

I started out the door and big Sam hollered, "I'll be grindin' meal this coming Saturday. Come back and get some."

When I got to my truck, there stood two, neatly dressed, young, black men. They asked if I was the one that hunted with Jim Smith. I nodded, and they said that they were glad their daddy had a friend. I said, "Looks like ya'll done good for yourselves." They just laughed. I told them that I would check up on Jim from time to time.

They said they would come back in a month and help their daddy build a barn to hold his corn. They also told me that every fall they would be back to help their daddy kill hogs and gather his crop. And they had a favor to ask of me: would I talk to Jim about his oil well? The oldest one said, "He'll just get caught. He quit when John Henry passed away, but now with a good crop of corn, he may be tempted again." I told them that I would talk to Jim, but I could not promise anything. They gave me their phone numbers and said to call them any time, day or night.

Then I remember an old school bus that was for sale. I told them that Jim had a mobile home, so why not a mobile barn? I explained that the old school bus stripped of its seats would hold several bushels of corn. They got the address for the school bus. They went and bought the bus and moved it to the old-house place that day.

A couple of months later, Jim got word to me to come and go coon hunting with him. I really didn't want to go coon hunting, but it would be a good time to talk to Jim about not moon shining anymore.

I got to Jim's just as it started to get dark. Jim was ready. We walked to the south field. The moon was full. It was light enough to walk without a flashlight. I talked to Jim about his *oil wells*. I reminded him of how he had felt pinned up while living at the apartments. I told him that if he got caught making moonshine, he would go to prison, where he would be pinned up for sure—where he could not even go outside the walls. Jim said that he had a good life now and that he would just leave it that way.

Old Red was well ahead of us. He barked just one short bark. He and some deer must have met head-on. The startled deer headed for the south field where Jim and I were. Seeing us, he turned to the left. The moonlight was shinning enough that we could see the white stripe.

Together, in almost a whispered reverence, we just said, "Forked Horn."

We both knew that Ol' Forked Horn would come back. This had always been his home. He was born here, and when he dies, it will probably be within a mile of here.

When we got back to the truck and started on our way to Jim's house, he told me that he had all that he wanted and that there would not be any new *oil wells*.

He said that he had to look out for John Henry and that ol' buck.

When I started home, I had just gotten to the locked gate when a rabbit hopped into the road. The rabbit stood up on its hind legs. It just stood there, looking at me. I opened the truck door, and the rabbit wiggled its ears and hopped away. If I had not known better, I would have sworn that it was John Henry, just hopping by to say "howdy."

I drove through, and as I closed the gate, I closed the tale of Ol' Forked Horn.

www.ingramcontent.com/pod-product-compliance
Lightning Source LLC
Chambersburg PA
CBHW021238280526
45784CB00005B/2143